Into The Light

Emily Stroia

Into the Light
Copyright © Emily Stroia, 2017
All rights reserved.

Book design: Stewart Williams
Cover art: jakegfx

Printed in the United States of America.
ISBN: 978-1-387-31517-8

Without limiting the rights under the copyright reserved above, no part of this publication may be reproduced, stored in, or introduced into a retrieval system, or transmitted in any form or by any means (electronic, mechanical, photocopying, recording, or otherwise) without prior written permission of the owner of this book.

For permission requests, please visit www.emilystroia.com.

*Dedicated to my younger self.
You are never alone & I will always love you.*

*The flower that blooms in adversity is the
most rare and beautiful of all.*

Table Of Contents

PART I: THE WOMB..1

PART I: THE BEGINNING...5

PART III: THE BREAKAWAY..43

PART IV: JOURNEY..63

PART V: BREAKTHROUGH..93

PART VI: FORGIVENESS..117

PART VII: TRUTH...129

PART I

The Womb

In the beginning I was light.
In the beginning I AM.
In the beginning the universe and I co-created.
A cosmic collective conversation on the nature of my being.
On the story that would be the container of my breakthrough.
Of my emergence.
On the guardians to carry me. Guide me.
Be the vessel of love and creation.
To greet me upon my arrival.
Before I was the flesh.
I signed the contract that would be the torch of my human experience.

"Who are you, Emily?" God asked.
"A beautiful, powerful, courageous woman."
"And so you are. Are you willing to do whatever it takes?"
"I AM."

"And so it is."

In the womb I was carried for nine months.
In conversation with God about my arrival.

From the heavens, I carried my angel wings with me down.
To a place called Earth.
To meet.
To know.
To heal.

In the womb I knew my soul as greatness.
I knew I carried many gifts that I would give and receive.

In the womb for the first time I heard the murmur of my mother's voice.
I heard the great struggle of life
and I was faced with the choice to abort my arrival.
To go or to stay?

What lies ahead is not for the light or easy.

"Do you choose to stay?" a voice echoed to me in the fetal position.

And in that moment, I arrived.

PART II

The Beginning

I have a request.
Can I share my story with you?
Will you promise to honor it?
To hold it & keep it safe?
And when it's time to bring it alive, will you be by my side when it's born?
When the world sees it for the first time?
This is a most delicate & sensitive process.
Going into the rooms of the House of the Past.
Talking to the ghosts that have haunted me for years.
I'm ready to share these secrets with you.
I'm ready to open the box.
Hold my hand as we begin.

I can't clearly recall the actual look
but I remember the feeling.
In this house I played.
In this house I climbed the trees
with a teddy bear I carried everywhere.
Together we played make-believe
in the world where the wild things are.
I loved playing make-believe.

In this house, my first word was fear.

I remember my mother crying many nights.
She often cried out of fear.
Memories of my father hitting her
crouched on the floor.
Holding herself. Holding her head.
In the fetal position.
I prayed he would stop.
I screamed for her.

In memory. In kindergarten.

It was a bad fight.
My mom screamed.
We walked down the metal stairs.
She seemed disoriented, confused.
She gave me $5.

It was the first time I received a $5 bill.

I had thought receiving money would feel exciting.
But this.
This felt cheap.
This felt confusing.

What was I supposed to do with $5?

I couldn't run to the candy store.
It was too late.
Besides, we were already running from my dad.

In memory, she was always running from him.

The unknown is like the space
between the
heartbeat.

I fell to my knees.

Blood covered me from head to toe.

"Mom, Dad, help!" I screamed.

The space of waiting. Hoping. Eternity flashed by in those minutes.

Helpless.

And slowly, step by step down, my mother emerged with her nightgown inside out.

My father, behind her, swooped up my brother with one arm.

Shattered glass everywhere.

I was in tears. In blood. In shock.

My mother stepped in and gently picked me up from the floor.

Carried me up the stairs to nurse my wounds.

My father held my brother.

"What happened to my bottle?" he asked curiously.

Moon child
where do you play?
In the stars
beneath the Milky Way?
Moon child
listen to the heartbeat
in the cosmic womb of the universe.
Wrap yourself safe inside
and stay.

Walking between the planes of the past and now.
I saw his eyes in another man's yesterday.
He held my hands as I shared the story of him and me.
I tasted the tears of his scars against me.
I could see my 12-year-old self in his eyes.
I carried his violations.
"It was all my fault,"
my mind whispered.
I can't tell the story without telling this story.
I stared at my father's eyes through another man's yesterday.

My nail polish is chipping.
A faint pink representing gentleness, my soft feminine.
The intimate side of me.
I play with this softness.
Tender and innocent.
There is a space I want to take you today.
It's by far the darkest place.
I still have nightmares.
Still haunted by the fear that lurked by me in the middle of the night.
I remember being 13.

The truth is
my father fell in love with me.
I wish I could go around the core of the story.
Hide the parts that don't make sense.
I was 13.

Looking for comfort from my mother's illness.
She would often pace the house in a navy blue winter coat.

Looking for comfort from my mother's illness.
She would often pace the house in a navy blue winter coat.

Talking to herself about how the world was against her.

They are watching me.
"Who, Mom?"
Everyone. Millionaire Martin.

Millionaire Martin was a man she became obsessed with.
Convinced he had spread rumors about her.
I wanted nothing more than for her to be normal.

To be a mom.
To talk to me about boys, school, and my friends.
But she was missing.

Aliens had abducted her.
In her mind, Satan was whispering in her ear.

Telling her to do things.
To end her life.
She didn't matter.
No one cared about her.
No one wanted her.
No one loved her.
Mom.

My love,
come up for air.
Let the light in.
Heartbreak opens doors.
Let the shadows out.
From the cocoon into transformation.
Sliding out from the layers.
The tethered web of stories.
Dance with them, my love.
Inside each box, we will piece together the picture.
One by one we open them.
This is the sacred home of your soul.
Don't hide
your scars.
We are carrying you home.
—From, the angels

I've been in a past playland
with my mother.
Bearing witness to her spirit.
To her love for me as a child.
We had a favorite game we would play.

I was probably around the age of 11 or 12 when we first started the game.
She was obsessed with women who had more.
More than one personality.

The Three Faces of Eve.
Sybil.
Mommie Dearest.
Flowers in the Attic.

She was searching for herself in them.
For answers to what was really wrong inside.

Every week we'd meet in the attic.
She would lay across from me on the couch. And we'd play.

I was her therapist, Dr. Mending.
There to help mend what she couldn't.

Excited to be a grown-up
I played Dr. Mending with conviction.

"How are you feeling today?" I'd ask.
"I'm okay, I had a fight with my husband this week," she'd reply.

"Okay, and who do we have with us today?"
"Barbara wants to talk today."

In her world of many we would search for the missing answers.

How did she lose her way?
How could we bring all of her back as one?

My mother is meek.
She hides her voice.
She waits for him to tell her she is worthy.
My mother shows me all the flaws in being a woman
and how to fall in love
with the wrong man.
My mother's ways still live inside me
in how I talk
in my anxiety.
Her gifts of writing
and intuition still guide me.
My mother taught me that the journey
of being a woman
is not always of a straight line.
Her rebel spirit
reminds me
that I am her daughter.
My mother is the woman
who taught me
how to live life with love
unapologetically.

*Find your power in
vulnerability
Find your voice in
truth
Find yourself in
love*

All wild things
give
and
grow
freely

I remember waking up in the middle of the night
screaming,
gasping for air.
A shadow often appeared
by my bedside
like the Grim Reaper
ready to collect me,
to take what didn't belong to him.
I remember not wanting to fall asleep
wondering what I'd wake up to:
him lying beside me
or my own nightmares.
Praying to God
that one day
I'd wake up
to light
and the darkness
of the night
would fade away.

We played with dolls.

I was seven.

"What happened with Mom & Dad this week?" she'd ask.

Boy Doll meets Girl Doll,

Boy Doll hits Girl Doll.

Dad hits Mom,

Mom cries.

They both fall down.

She'd pace in circles.
Room to room.
Talking out loud,
making sense of the voices
in her head.
God?
Are you there?
I think the devil is talking to me.
Do you hear them too?

Night talks
with the ocean.
She shared her secrets of
love and pain.
I sobbed
broke open my heart
released my tears
in her waves' grace.
Mother Moon appeared
from the clouds
in her light.
A message shined.
Even after the darkness
there is still so much
light.

Life together wasn't always bad.
There were moments of light too.
Shared the stories of our ancestors.
Ate the food that nourished our spirits & bellies.
Old jokes that brought warmth to our hearts.
Fights that ended in tears & laughter.
Played in the sun,
fed the ducks.
Made road trips to the ocean.
Awkward hugs.
AC/DC. The Doors. Jimi Hendrix.
These were the days of our lives together.
This was our family.

Don't tell me
I don't matter.
I am yours,
therefore I matter.

I prayed for a miracle.
It arrived in the form of a prayer.
God grant me the serenity to accept
the things
I cannot change
the courage to change the things I can
and the wisdom to know the difference.

I guess I was always a fighter
I fought hard until the very end
I left
kissed them goodbye.
My heart broke
into a million pieces
opened the cage
my spirit was in
into the light
into the wind
wild & free.

He lay beside me
my budding breasts
soft skin.
Deep in the night
his head quietly fell
next to my pillow.
My 13-year-old self
never spoke
about our secret
of what he said
of what he wanted
of the nights
he spent
beside me.

All I can remember
is what he took:
my gentleness
my grace
my power
my womanhood
my voice

*My love,
come up for air.
Let the light in.*

A punch to the face
a blow to the head
blood on my lips
cries for help...

Where was God on that day?
An explosion that broke
the universe
that held together
the last thread
of our family.

I walked with them through the sands of time. . .
their faint outlines in the distance
I followed their light
hoping I could see their faces

This is the place we created our story
that would span for centuries
she smiled back at me
trusting I'd be always right behind her

singing her sweet song calling out to me
never once letting go
her child
her love

I believed in magic
at night the universe and I would talk
In the morning, I found my breath
my inner voice
a gentle whisper
the sun's rays on my face
and the hope that a miracle would arrive
to guide my way

I was sweet
like the honeysuckle
that grows wild in the summer
and he, the taker who stole my sweetness
turned it
sour

I created my
own wonderland
where he couldn't touch me
where they couldn't find me
where all was well
and I was safe
loved
and light
nothing could
hurt me
in this space

Heartbreak opens doors.
Let the shadows out.

What would it take
for them
to remember
the gift
life gave them,
the angel
that arrived
in their arms

I played in the trees
talked to the leaves.
I was always a magical child
with unique superpowers.
I could see. Feel. Know
moments
before they happened.
In school they called me "gifted."
I always knew
there was something
different
about me.

One day
the stars
shared a message with me
what was happening to me
was not to me
but for me
I would share my gifts
with the world
I arrived with purpose
with intention
to heal
beyond measure
beyond light years
to reconnect and
to love
even the most unlovable

My mother had
pearl-white skin
soft green eyes
a gap in between her two front teeth
dimples every time she smiled
cracked skin on her hands
blistered fingers.
Addicted to
caffeine & cigarettes.
A keeper of her children
a writer of poems.
She wore her heart on her sleeve
gave whatever she had away
asked for nothing and
desired only one thing:
true love.

I remember the journal
that held the stories
of my late-night fears
uncried tears
This was my best friend
who kept my secrets
and made me feel safe
In its pages
I found solace
and the trust
to know
everything would be okay

PART III

The Breakaway

Let go of everything.

Find it all
when nothing
is left.

My intuition
guided me
to a new home
where I could find myself
far away
from everything
that broke me

The silence
was enough
to shatter
the earth
into a
million pieces

There is a message
even in the
silence

He promised
this time it would be different.
He found me
behind the walls
I built
to keep him out.
We went for a drive that day.
I saw that same look in his eyes
from years ago.
He turned to me
whispered in my ear,
"Some things never change."
My heart panicked.
I reached for the door
never to turn back
to speak
again.

In the night
my mind
wandered in the labyrinths
of then
now
and
how

How to heal
how to let go
how to know
it was safe
to love
again

In my meditations
I found a curiosity
a space
to heal

A space
to
LOVE

A space
for
safety

In my meditations
I heard
the nudges
of my own
inner voice:

TRUST
TRUST
TRUST

From the cocoon into transformation.
Sliding out from the layers.
The tethered web of stories.
Dance with them, my love.

Love is
risking getting your heart
broken
again and again

In the hurt
you find
yourself.
In the hurt
you find
the truth.
In the hurt
you find
the strength
of your being.

I get my fighter spirit from my father.
And, in some ways, he made me tougher than I needed to be—
harder, less connected, but crazy, passionate, and wild as fire.

I remember his cold words
and painful actions.
The scars on my hands & feet always remind me.

My thoughts wander to the day when I will lay our story
to rest.
How my heart will break but my spirit, free.

I am peaceful.
I am wild.
I am both at the same time.
And I have him to thank for it.
For even in the memories I can still find meaning
in this journey
called life.

*Who were you
before
it
happened?*

It may break you
in ways you never knew.
It may haunt you
in every corner
of your mind.
You may find
yourself
running
in a maze
only to return
to where it all began.

This is where
you and the darkness
meet
to find
the light
again.

Before I knew
the truth
about what he wanted
I loved him
like the man
he could be
Before I knew
what he came for
he was everything
to me

Do me a favor:
Leave your heart open.
You are at your most beautiful
when you let go and surrender.
All that is waiting for you is within you.

In a vision
I was guided
to a sanctuary by the sea.
In a vision
a Great Spirit
found me.
In a vision
I discovered the answer
in the veins of life
to what could
set me f r e e.
What had been missing: M E.
Before I found me
I was broken.
Before I found me
I was finding ways
to shake myself
from the cage
I hid in.
Before I found me
I was lost in space that wasn't me.

One more
broken promise.
One more
lie
to keep
the hope
of us
alive.
One more
cruel word
to remind me
he still cared.
One more slap
to know
he would always
be there.

A rainbow appeared.
Showed its face so bright
it cleared
the clouds of the past,
the rainstorms of chaos.
The miracle I prayed for
had finally arrived.

*I know life hasn't been easy.
Humans aren't always kind.*

*Before you let life harden you
open your heart
one more time.*

PART IV

Journey

How could I find
peace
when the shadows of the night
were so loud
inside of me?

*What did you give
to the world
that you forgot
to give
to yourself?*

*Inside each box we will piece
together the picture.
One by one we open them.
This is the sacred home of
your soul.*

I thought he could save me.
I thought she could save me.
I thought a new home would heal me,
only to discover
I was the only one
who could
save me.

We said goodbye
a thousand times
before his marks on me
became so much
that I
even forgot
who I was
without him

He said,
"I'm sorry
I hit you.
You just make me so angry."

"I thought it was
the only way
I'd receive his love,"
she cried.

"How you been?"
he asked timidly.

[Fearful.
Unable to sleep.
I don't trust anyone.
I cheat.
I hurt people.
I have nightmares.
I hide.
I drink too much.
I bailed on therapy last week.]

"Good, everything's great,"
I replied.

On the floor
the years of the past
shattered.
She watched the memories of
their life dance before her.
Here
the light bled in.
It was time
to face
what she had been running from.
To face the truth
To face the face
that still haunted her in
the middle of the night.

I listen and watch.
The sense of innocence stolen.
In the air.
I know the feeling all too well.
I see my 13-year-old self in her.
I wish I could turn back time.
To when she felt safe.
To when life didn't terrify her so.
I pray her fears don't eat her alive.
Or the night terrors begin to haunt her.
Like they did me.
Beyond time and memory.
I pray she will come out braver.
Stronger.
Brighter.
Reminded of my own soft pain.
I reflect on the memories of days when innocence wasn't lost.
And life was sweet.
Playground days.

In the search
for myself
I discovered
space
silence
spirit
healing
and
MY INTUITION

What's holding you back?

*Let
it
go.*

Father
Mother
Brother
The silence
between the words
I know it's hard
to say what we really feel
to love how we want to
let go
and heal

I recycled his love
and gave it to someone else.
I hurt them
the way he hurt me
because I thought
that's how love
was supposed to be.

When he promised he'd come
I waited.
When he promised he'd stop calling me names
I listened.
When he said he wouldn't hit me anymore
I hoped.
And when he said he'd change
I believed.

My heart called.
She said she was ready
to stop fighting.
But then I heard the sound of his voice.
Saw the scars on my skin.
And felt my heart sink
one more time.
My tears are the only things
I can't stop fighting.

Love,
you are the greatest gift
I have ever received.
Love,
you bring life
to all the broken parts
of me.
Love,
you have healed
my heart
in ways I could never see.
Love,
you have awakened a fire
and liberated me.

On the quest for peace
my intuition
led me
in a vision
to the tree of life.
I found
a Great Spirit who sat across from me,
whispered softly:
to heal is to give,
to receive is to love,
to know is to trust,
to surrender is to feel
peace.

But why would it make sense
to forgive
the unforgivable?
How could I
when every night
I was reminded
of his skin next to mine
pretending to protect me
when all along
it was him
I needed protection from?

We go in circles.
He calls.
I hang up.
Swearing I will never call him again.
But my heart softens.
Memories remind me
of what I miss most.
Months go by.
I pray he changed.
I pray this time it will be different.
I call.
A dial tone.
Just the faint memory of a tiny space
of when I could feel
him breathing beside me.

I've beat myself up
thinking I wasn't enough for him.
I bent.
Shifted.
Hid.
Spoke up.
Kept quiet.
Laughed when he said so.
Whatever made him happy.
I gave up my soul
kept myself
black & blue
bruised
to be connected
to him.

Every day
I woke up
struggling
to find my power
to find my voice.
He was living inside my head.
His words echoed in the air I breathed,
in the conversations I had.
All I wanted
was to be free
from the nightmares
of his spirit
haunting me
reminding me
of all
that I couldn't see.

My last ray of hope
died.
Some time ago.
I've been climbing over and under
cracking through walls
of pain
I've carried
since my mother's womb.
The fighter in me
has surrendered.

Even she has laid her weapons
to rest.
I walked in faith
with my eyes closed yesterday.
Listening to the sounds of the city
beside me.

Blindly feeling around
for the rainbow that's promised.

In the dark
it takes trust
to keep walking.

Here's the story:
my therapist tells me of a woman walking in the desert.
Dragging a trunk behind her.
With every step she takes, the trunk becomes heavier.
And eventually unbearable to carry.
A man walks by and asks,
"Ma'am, what are you carrying in the trunk that you can't let go of?"
She replies,
"My father."

Let go.

Conversations with the past
come up in my visions.
I fight to find
forgiveness.
I want so badly
to forgive him
to tell him
how much I think of him
but my heart
whispers,
"Not yet."
So I wait
for him to apologize
to right all of his wrongs.
But even in my visions
he is still the same.

My love,
when will you change?

It wasn't God who saved her.
It wasn't anyone
but timing.
My phone rang
in the night.
The woman who had been my saving grace
decided her soul wasn't ready
to live in the shadows
of this Earth
and so the darkness overcame her.

And her razor slid like a violin on her wrist.

In the hospital that became her sanctuary.
Letting go of all the stories in my head
about her. About him.
I rushed to be by her side.
It had been years.

And for the first time.
She looked at me with her soft green eyes
with a look of deep apology
and a spark of hope
that we'd find a way for her to find healing
to find peace
from the demons living inside her.
Deep breaths. I held her in my arms.
A miracle took place in our hearts
and the light began to find its way in.

I am being submerged
under the well
of my own tears
talking to the fears
that hold me
sleepless nights
listening
the universe speaks
in a myriad of ways
I'm coming undone
there are no more rooms
I can hide in
surrendering, I collapse
an angel appears
she carries me
knowing
the strong don't always survive
she carries me home

I wanted her to know
that I'd always be there.
I sprinkled my light on her heart
left a little bit of magic
to remind her
that she is never alone
she is never forgotten.
I carry her love
with me.
Left her a letter:

"Always together
just close your eyes
and
know that I am there
in all the spaces
between the breath and your heartbeat."

—Mother and daughter

He said I'd never make it,
that I was worthless.
All these years I spent fighting to prove him wrong.
All these years I spent running from him.
I blamed it on our past.
Gave my power away
forgot my voice.
I woke up ready
to face the woman in the mirror
and love her again.
Because hating him was too heavy to carry.
Because loving me is everything.
Because letting go became the only option.
I laid down my weapons and surrendered the war inside my head.
Let go and
led with my heart instead.

PART V

Breakthrough

In the breakdown
the way
appears
In the breakthrough
remain
the answers

In a dream…they screamed
"Fight for your life!"
but what
is there to fight for
when I feel so dead inside?
How can I go on
when the only heart I can't feel
is my own?

The nightmares
The fear of him touching me
I cried in pain
holding myself
holding my heart
All the darkness that lay deep
in my bones
in my blood
in my breath
I wanted to be free
I needed to be free
It was this or nothing
My heart knew more
Crouched in the fetal position
slowly I let out
the years of madness
one scream at a time
YOU, my past
won't win this time
I came to fight
to take back my soul
It's not yours to live on anymore
This darkness
no longer gets to breathe inside of me
Reached out from the depths and transformed
the monsters of the night
into light

And so we go back and forth
me and the past
dancing through time
feeling every memory
every scar.
My higher self asked,
"Do you want to hold onto that?"

"But it's all I know," my mind whispered.

The shards of glass
lay beneath me
"Drown out her screams with this"
A bathroom hand towel in my mouth
blood on my hands
The day it all changed
I prayed for a miracle
and the universe listened
Life spoke
the Earth shook
violently
Mother Earth rose up
reminding me of the light
deep inside my heart
of the story that would birth itself
into the world
to awaken consciousness
to a new awareness: that we all matter

*Just breathe and lean
into my arms*

Mother Earth sent her angels
to walk beside me

A fire that burns so bright
not even he could touch it

Don't give up

I won't give up
My story is the change
I want to see in the world

The Great Spirits came to deliver a message:
"There is nothing left here for you.
You have been to the wasteland
in the rooms of the past.
But only what you see is the dark.
Breathe light into them
and then you will see light."

*When you are at the end of
your rope,
tie a knot and hold on.
When you think you are at the
end of your journey,
reach out your hand
and someone will meet you
there.*

*Don't hide
your scars.
We are carrying you
home.*

*—Love,
The angels*

In the quiet
I think
of you,
my love.
What you look like
what you feel like.
How long
until our eyes
meet.
The rain falls sweetly
reminding me
that true love
takes time.
My heart aches
to know your name.
I wonder...
can you hear me
call for you,
my love?

Honor the feelings.
All the feelings.
Give them a voice.
The rage.
The hurt.
The love. Confusion. Fear.
Let them live so they know they matter.
Let them come. And let them go.
They are the beauty even in the madness.
Love them. All of them.

And so I was given an ultimatum.
My higher self called.
In my sleep she awakened me.
Shouted so loudly I had no other choice.
She showed me all the doors to the past.
Invited me to walk through them.
"Visit as long as you want
but remember you really only have one choice."
Leave.
Leave it all behind.
Your choice.

If you stay your soul will suffocate.
Let your heart break if you must.
Do whatever it takes.
But, my dear, the only way out is through.
Open your heart.
Let your soul breathe again.

I walked through the doors.
I walked back into the House of the Past.
Sat with the memories that haunted me.
Felt myself fall apart piece by piece.
Like the phoenix that rises from the ash.
I stood in the fire.
Every tear burned slowly down my cheek.
The universe bellowed into the depths of my core,
"ARE YOU READY?
ARE YOU READY TO LET GO?"

And there I stood.
Falling to my knees.
Crying in fear.
Feeling the pain rise in my body.
Like a volcano slowly ready to erupt.

Every cell in my body.
Awoke from a deep sleep.
And in a split second a force greater than me, a power as deep as the ocean.
A voice I had never heard before screamed a thousand cries.

There it was. The voice I had been looking for all these years.

"What took you so long?" my heart cried.

The burning fire faded.
My body softened.
My soul quieted.
My hands held my heart.
And my voice reverberated its arrival in all the cells of my being.
The sound of the voice I hid was finally here.

She asked me,
"So what binds you still to the past?"

(What kind of question is that?
I'm not still tied to the past.)

"Shame.

That I will disappoint them one more time."

My father's words echo in my head.

You just don't leave your family.
You never turn your back on your family.

"This might be my last chance.
Isn't it wrong that I am not close to them?"

"The truth of the matter is that I think I am just not worth it.
That's what binds me to the past."

All the thoughts I had never shared
found their way out.

"It's not about living a happy life,
it's about living a real one," she replied.

And that's the thing about pain.
It comes and it goes.
Like waves.
Ebbs and flows.
It's still.
And quiet.
Loud. Tumultuous.
A beast.
A force of nature
that wants to be heard.
Given a voice.
To be held.
Softly,
without question,
without judgment.
In love.
With time.
And space.

I lay there
for a while
in full surrender.
They came to me in a vision.
Dressed in light.
Higher than their earthly selves.
For a few minutes I felt full, immense love for them.
For a few seconds I understood them.

Time showed me what it was like to forget the past.
I realized their souls were unwell.
Torn and frayed.
Fighting for an anchor to something
Besides darkness.

I wanted to pause everything.
Hold them in that light.

But they were untouchable.
Impenetrable.
And just as fast as they came

they were gone.

The stories I've been living in:
I'm not enough
I'm not worthy
I'm unlovable
Not deserving

The stories I'm letting go of:
I'm not enough
I'm not worthy
I'm unlovable
Not deserving

The stories I'm embracing:
I am enough
I am worthy
I am lovable
I am deserving

She screamed a thousand times,
"It's because you're not open!
You don't give things a chance."

I've been staring out the window watching the leaves
change.
I've replayed her words in my mind.
Trying to find a new meaning to them.
Trying to put the pieces together differently.
Because maybe, just maybe,
I'll feel better about the truth.

The truth of who I am inside.
A message not just from her.
But from a deeper place. . .
I saw myself in her that day.

A reflection of myself
screaming at me.
A message that reverberated in the universe.
The leaves aren't the only things changing.

I fought hard to stay attached.
Attached to the story.
Attached to the only form of connection we had.
It was safer.
Familiar.
I knew the feeling all too well.
But when I surrendered
all the feelings I had been hiding from appeared.
Liberation.
Growth.
Joy.
Innocence.
Freedom.
And me.

It has become uncomfortable living here.
This house has gotten old.
It's time.
Time to let it all go.

So I called them forth in a vision.
Called a conference with their souls.
The great masters stood around us.
Held us in light.
As we gathered to meet again.
Different yet the same.
I looked deeply in their eyes.
My voice shook.
My body trembled.

In thought we conversed.
"Where have you been?"
"Hiding in the shadows?"

I had finally given the pain a voice.

I took their hands.
My Earth guides.
The guardians of my life.
With their touch and with their hearts
they showed me in visions
that danced before me.
The greatest memories.
The broken parts.
The anger.
The silence.
Our fiery love for one another.

All that they could have done.
All their regrets.
All that they did.

And all that they left behind for me.

My greatest teachers.
My greatest loves.
My greatest healers.
The change agents of the universe.

"Time is up," the masters shouted.

Remembering all that was.
And all that is.
All that will always be.

Carrying the messages from our ancestors.
Healing the scars of the past.
Stepping into the greatness of our love.

A new story to be told.
A new legacy to be created.
Our souls forever connected.

And in the light we faded away.

In the breakthrough
you will first face the breakdown of breakdowns.
The rise and fall
of the great walls you've built around your heart.
The cracks in the armor
you've walked around in.
In the breakthrough
you will experience all the prisons of the past.
Shake. Tremble. Fall apart.
Piece by piece.
Fall to your feet. Bow in mercy
and curtsy as you rise to your greatness.
In the breakthrough you will first
go to war
before finding your greatest peace.
In the breakthrough
you will feel the last release, the last rupture,
the last shriek & cry.
You will lay down your weapons
and surrender.

PART VI

Forgiveness

Forgiveness is letting go
of the story of how it should be.
Accept what was.
Surrender the fight,
loving the dark & the light.

We've both hurt each other.
Cursed each other's names.
Wished we'd never met.
Walked away.
Stood in our silent bitter rage.
The return to love is not always easy.

Forgiving is for healing.

"Come back to love," the universe requested.

We were asked to give up our stories.
And remember we are the same.
There is no difference, not even in our rage.

All that is left is remembering, surrendering, and trusting
that a new beginning starts the moment
we embrace change.

Years later, I called him
to say all the things I'd been wanting to say.

My voice quivered.

I had punished him by not:
    1. Reaching out.
    2. Saying I love you.
    3. Staying in the stories of our past.
    4. Letting go and giving him my power.

What I wanted to say:
    1. There was never a day he didn't cross my mind.
    2. I tried to put our past away in the corners of my mind.
    3. I avoided him. I avoided us.
    4. The real truth: that I missed him.

Little breaks.
Soft touches.
Gentle voices.
Hearts still.
The beating of our love
carries us back.
Like a river it flows.
Slowly back into each other's arms.
Back to our roots.
Back
home.

Turn your face
towards the light
and let the shadows walk beside you

I think
I love him
but right now
I am trying
to love me
more

To be complete.
To be whole.
Is to be one with it all.
To know each story and love it
love it all the same.

The story doesn't change.
You do.

We are each other's greatest healers.
Let your story be the guide.

The darkness is just darkness.
The light is just light.
And you,
you are the magic that brings it all alive.

You might want to hold on a little longer.
You might think it's not safe.

Don't confuse forgiveness with anything else.
It's simply the knowledge it couldn't have been any
other way.

Love the scars of your past.
Let them be the reminders of how
you survived.
Of how you conquered
and found a new way.

PART VII

Truth

He lies
next to me
as we surrender
to the morning light.
The gifts of the sun
shine brightly
bringing love
to my heart,
showing light
where shadows
used to be.
Discovering the sun
all along
was inside me.

Can you live
in faith
knowing
there are no promises
in the unknown
or will you
walk back to the
familiar
where life feels safe?
You get to decide.
The blindfold
is merely
a guide.
Whatever your choice,
your eyes
will be opened
or
closed.

In the microlayers of my being
is the subtle voice
that gives
that gently nudges
me
to the truth of who I am.
Pause.
Breathe.
Listen.
In the stillness I find the answers.

You are LOVE.

Beyond measure.

Beyond doubt.

Love is giving
unconditionally

Healing talks
Our past
falls away
Love her still
Love her always

I am letting go of being all things
and coming back to the being of it all
Me

Your light
and your dark
are both beautiful

I stopped living.
Living in our stories.
Released my resentments.
Told him the truth.
Took my power back.
And set us both free.

There is an invisible thread that will forever keep us connected.
In life and death.
I will always remember him
hold him close.
Keep us in my heart.
The only ghost I want to remember is the love we shared.

If you ever wonder what you could have done differently
remember you were doing your best
with what you knew how

I have come to the end of this story.
The one where they hurt me.

And where I hurt them
because of it.

I am done with this story.
With the cycle and recycle of the past.

A new story is arriving.
And while the words are still coming to life,

I know that our story
ends with love.

Into the House of Past I journeyed again
talked with the skeletons that haunted me.
Made peace with the Hows.
Let go of the Whys.
Said goodbye to old endings.
Closed the door behind me.
Created a new beginning.

Searched long and far to find her.
Called out her name in my dreams.
Saw her in my meditations.
Wondered if we'd ever meet.

And then one day I woke up.
Walked into the bathroom.
Stared in the mirror.
My eyes reflected back a light.
Reflected back a soul.
The soul I was searching for
all along
was me.

In the web of your past
microlayers of truth hide.
Your self will trick you
into believing a story that may be all lies.
In your search find
the space between the dark and the light.
Where peace meets with past.
Where power meets with life.
And where you meet your light.

You are the greatest gift anyone could ever receive.
Be that gift to yourself.

Power is not just finding your voice
but letting your voice
be heard

Finding space in the breath.
Talking to the sun.
Listening with my core.
A new chapter is beginning.
A new home is building
the past, healing.
Deep in the layers of my soft and tender heart
after all these years
I have
arrived.

So dance if your heart wants to dance.
Cry if your heart wants to cry.
Sing if your heart wants to sing.
And most importantly, love.
Love
if your heart wants to Love.

When you feel the past leave you
a rebirth will happen.
Your heart will crack open
and your being will remember
what it lost.
Your true self will awaken
from its sleep.
And your soul will dance
calling forward all the gifts you left behind.
And you, the phoenix, will rise again.

And one day
a crack in the story:
the fear of letting go
was no longer as great
as the fear of holding on

Show me all the places where you hide
so I can hold you there

Fall in love with your heart. Your one
sweet
precious
tender Heart.

Calm your madness
by finding stillness.
Acknowledge it.
Give it its own name.
Let it run wild
like the child you once were.
Once you do, your madness will no longer
be madness,
but instead,
freed.

When I look at you
I see something
I have never seen before.
The world has done you wrong.
But you are magic despite and because of it.

Thank you for being a witness to my journey.
Even in the shadows. Holding me in the spaces between.
I see you. I feel you.
I am asking you to pay it forward.
Let your voice be heard.
Share your dark with the world.
Let it become your light.
You are a gift and someone is waiting to know you.
I will always be cheering you on.
Let your story be your guide.

—From my heart to yours.